ALLEN COUNTY PUBLIC LIBRARY
3 1833 03073 8030

The Society of Mareen Duvall Descendants

Md. Historical Soc.

HOLY TRINITY CHURCH
Near Collington, Maryland
June 30, 1929

Hood, John

The Duvall family. [Baltimore?] The Society of Mareen Duvall Descendants, 1929.

30 p., illus., geneal.table 21½ cm.

50334(copy 1)
2 copies(keep both for more complete information)

1.Duvall fam. 2.Holy Trinity Church,near Collington,Md. 3.Society of Mareen Duvall Descendants.

This booklet contains the genealogy of the Duvall family which was (according to tradition) founded by MAREEN DUVALL, the French Huguenot, who came to America and settled in Maryland in the year 1659—an additional sketch of Holy Trinity Church near Collington, Maryland, where the Duvall descendants met July 24, 1927 to honor their distinguished Ancestor—and a copy of the Will of Mareen Duvall is also given which is recorded in the Land Office at Annapolis, Md.

HOLY TRINITY CHURCH, Near Collington, Maryland, June 30, 1929

The Duvall Family

By the late Dr. John Hood

Baltimore, Maryland

FRENCH Pedigree.—Duvall—Noble family, originally of Beaumont le Roger in Normandy, who held in the twelfth century the fief or estates Duvall, situated in that province.

I. Hugh Duvall, Esq., (equerry), Sir Duvall, the best known of this name, married Adilena—issue Robert, Jane, who married Guy de Beauveon, in favor of which marriage Robert Duvall, her brother, relinquished to her among other things the fief of Duvall, by letters or deeds given in the year 1298.

II. Robert Duvall married the Honorable Lady Jane de Pritot, and had among other issue:

III. John Duvall, knight, lord so called of the place, who lived in 1375, as appears from letters given the same year, June 2, before or in the presence of Daudouin de St. Paul, knight and keeper of warren, of waters and forests.

IV. Lawrence Duvall, Esq., married the noble Lady Agnes de Marmien, who brought as a marriage portion lands and lordships in the province of St. Peter.

V. William Duvall, Esq., lord, etc., married Alex. de Mamusin and had issue—Massiot and others.

VI. Massiot Duvall, lord, province St. Lawrence and of the fief of St. Aubin, married Margaret de Orbin, had issue:

VII. Thomas Duvall, Esq., lord of Ange, in the province of St. Lawrence, and the fief St. Aubin, who married Nicola Stagard, from whom, through Mareen

[illegible] Peerage—Duvall—Noble Family, origin.
[illegible] arrived there about le Roger le Duvall, who held in [illegible] public court [illegible] the seignory Duvall, situated [illegible] that province.

I. Ralph Duvall, Esq., Seigneur of Duvall, the first [illegible] of this name, married Audoine [illegible] Lady, who married Guy de Beaumont in favor of which marriage Audoine Duvall, her mother, relinquished to her among other things the fief of Duvall, by letters or deeds given in the year 1238.

II. Robert Duvall married the Honorable Lady Jane de Prunet, and had among other issue:

III. John Duvall, knight, lord so called of the place, who lived in 1375, as appears from letters given the same year, June 4, before [illegible] in the presence of Bertrand de St. Paul, knight and lord [illegible] of [illegible] and [illegible].

IV. Lawrence Duvall, Esq., married the noble Lady Agnes de Montreuil, who brought as a marriage portion lands and lordships in the province of St. Malo.

V. William Duvall, Esq., lord, etc., married Alice de [illegible], and had issue Mervyn and others.

VI. Mervyn Duvall, lord, province St. Lawrence and of the fief of St. Aubin, married Margaret de Colion, and [illegible] son:

VII. Thomas Duvall, Esq., lord of Anon, in the province of St. Lawrence, and the fief St. Aubin, who married Nicole Sergent, [illegible], through Mervyn

Duvall, the Huguenot immigrant to Maryland, descend the distinguished family of that name.

* * *

As early as the year 1648 Cecilius Calvert instructed Gov. William Stone to give to any French, who were already settled, or who might thereafter be settled in the colony, all the rights and privileges enjoyed by the English and Irish immigrants, who alone up to that time enjoyed the rights of citizenship.

Acts for the denization of foreigners occur frequently in the early records. Many French Huguenots came into Maryland, but not in settlements, as did the Swedes and Dutch along the Delaware. In 1666 the council of State passed an act naturalizing French Protestants, whereby those who, like the Puritans of England and Catholics of England and Ireland, had left their native land for the sake of their religion, were received without persecution or restriction in the land of religious freedom.

Among the earliest and most prominent of the French Huguenots was Mareen Duvall, who arrived in Maryland early in 1659 and on August 28, 1659, a tract of land on the south side of South River in Anne Arundel county, near the site of New London, was surveyed and patented to him, under the name of "La Val," no doubt in memory of the family estates in France. His landed possessions soon included several thousand acres lying in Anne Arundel and Prince George counties. That this provident French refugee was of the Protestant faith is evident from the fact that he built, at his own expense, on his home plantation in the latter county a chapel for private worship. In the year 1705 his son, John Duvall, and his wife appeared before the vestry, of which he was a member, and deeded the land upon which the chapel stood to Queen Anne for the use of the parish, but it was not until the year 1741 that it became a parish

Englishmen and Irish immigrants, who alone up to that time enjoyed the rights of citizenship.

Acts for the denization of foreigners occur frequently in the early records. Many French Huguenots came into Maryland, but not in settlements, as did the Swedes and Dutch along the Delaware. In 1666 the Council of State passed an act naturalizing French Protestants, whereby those who, like the Pilgrims of England and Covenanters of Scotland and Ireland, had left their native land for the sake of their religion, were received without persecution or restriction in our land of religious freedom.

Among the earliest and most prominent of the French Huguenots was Mareen Duvall, who settled in Maryland early in 1659 and on August 25, 1659, a tract of land on the south side of South River in Anne Arundel county, near the site of New London, was surveyed and patented to him under the name of "La Val," as a tribute to the memory of the family estates in France. His landed possessions soon included several thousand acres lying in Anne Arundel and Prince George's counties. That this prominent French refugee was of the Huguenot faith is evident from the fact that he built, at his own expense, on his home plantation in the latter county a chapel for private worship. In the year 1709 his son, John Duvall, and his wife appeared before the vestry of which he was a member and deeded the land upon which the chapel stood to Queen Anne for the use of the parish, but it was not until the year 1741 that it became a parish

church, supported and repaired by the community, as up to that time it was maintained by the Duvall family.

* * *

Mary, the widow of Mareen Duvall the first, became the wife of the first rector of what is now Holy Trinity, near Collington, Prince George county, in Queen Anne parish, erected from St. Paul's in the year 1705. This Rev. Jacob Henderson, rector, married the widow of Col. Henry Ridgely and wife of the first Mareen Duvall. The church built so long ago by one who renounced home and country for the sake of religious freedom perpetuates the memory of its first patron in its memorial windows to the Duvall family. Mareen Duvall was a strong adherent of King James, as will be seen in Col. Nicholas Greenbury's letter to Gov. Lionel Copley, in which he calls the Governor's attention to the Jacobite cabal composed of Colonel Darnell, Samuel Chew, Edward Dorsey and others, and that a staunch Protestant, the latter was willing to associate with both Romanists and those of his own faith in loyal support of the rightful heir to the throne. In the year 1678, by act of assembly Mareen Duvall, with twenty-three other gentlemen, was appointed commissioner of Anne Arundel county to lay out and survey towns, ports, etc.

* * *

In an account given in provincial records of an Indian outbreak it is stated that the house of Mareen Duvall had to be especially guarded, but for what reasons is not stated. In the family record left by Mr. Justice Gabriel Duvall, a grandson of Mareen Duvall, the immigrant and his wife Susanna we find that he was born in 1752, and was a son of Benjamin Duvall, the youngest son of Mareen Duvall the first. This Gabriel Duvall was successively a commissioner of confiscated estates, member of Exeçutive Council, member of Legislature,

church, supported and repaired by the communicants, as in other wise it was maintained by the Duvall family.

* * *

Mary, the widow of Mareen Duvall the first, became the wife of the first rector of what is now Holy Trinity near Collington, Prince George county, in Queen Anne parish, erected from St. Paul's in the year 1705. The Rev. Jacob Henderson, rector, married the widow of Col. Henry Ridgely and wife of the first Mareen Duvall.

The church built so long ago by one who renounced home and country for the sake of religious freedom, perpetuates the memory of its first patron in commemorative windows to the Duvall family. Mareen Duvall was a strong adherent of King James, as will be seen in Col. Nicholas Greenberry's letter to Gov. Lionel Copley, in which he calls the Governor's attention to the Jacobite cabal composed of Colonel Darnall, Samuel Chew, Edward Dorsey and others, and that a scotch Protestant, the latter was willing to associate with both Romanists and those of his own kind in loyal support of the exiled heir to the throne. In the year 1696, by act of assembly Mareen Duvall, with twenty-three other gentlemen, was appointed commissioner of Anne Arundel county to lay out and survey towns, ports, etc.

* * *

In an account given in historical records of an Indian outbreak it is stated that the lands of Mareen Duvall had to be especially guarded, but by what means is not stated. In the family record left by Mr. Justice Gabriel Duvall, a grandson of Mareen Duvall, the immigrant and his wife [illegible] he said that he was born in 1752, and was a son of Benjamin Duvall, the youngest son of Mareen Duvall the first. This Gabriel Duvall was successively a commissioner [illegible], member of Executive Council, member of Legislature,

member of Congress, a Judge of the Supreme Court of Maryland, Comptroller of the Treasury of the United States from December 5, 1802, to November 21, 1811, and Associate Justice of the Supreme Court of the United States from 1811 to 1836.

Two of his brothers, Edward and Isaac, officers in the Maryland Line, the former killed in battle August 8, 1780, the latter at Eutaw Springs in the engagement of September, 1781.

Susannah Duvall, a daughter of the Huguenot refugee married Robert Tyler, the first of the name in America and from them descended President John Tyler, General Bradley Tyler Johnson, of the Confederate Army, and other distinguished persons.

Mary Duvall, another daughter of the first Mareen, married in 1701 the Rev. Henry Hall, of Horsham, England, the first rector of St. James' parish, Herring Creek, Anne Arundel County, appointed by the Bishop of London to that charge in the year 1698. Their descendants still worship and bury in this parish.

Other children of Mareen Duvall and his wife, were Mareen, called the elder, who married before the death of his father, 1694, Frances Stockett; Captain John, who married Elizabeth Jones, daughter of William Jones, Sr.; Eleanor, who married John Roberts, of Virginia; Lewis, who married Martha Ridgely, daughter of Robert, the colonial official. These children were by Mareen Duvall's first wife, whose name has never been discovered as he most likely married her before leaving France.

He married for his second wife Susannah ———, whose identity is also a mystery. His children by this wife were Mareen, called the younger, who married Elizabeth Jacobs, daughter of Capt. John Jacobs;

and Associate Justice of the Supreme Court of the United States from 1811 to 1836.

Two of his brothers, Edward and Isaac, officers in the Maryland Line, the former killed in battle August 8, 1780, the latter at Eutaw Springs in the engagement of September, 1781.

Susannah Duvall, a daughter of the Huguenot refugee, married Robert Tyler, the first of the name in America, and from them descended President John Tyler, General Bradley Tyler Johnson, of the Confederate Army, and other distinguished persons.

Mary Duvall, another daughter of the first Mareen, married in 1701 the Rev. Henry Hall, of Hertford, England, the first rector of St. James' parish, (Herring Creek), Anne Arundel County, appointed by the Bishop of London to that charge in the year 1698. Their descendants still worship and live in that parish.

Other children of Mareen Duvall and his wife were Mareen, called the elder, who married before the death of his father, 1694, Frances Stockett; Captain John, who married Elizabeth Jones, daughter of William Jones; Eleanor, who married John Roberts, of Virginia; Lewis, who married Martha Ridgely, daughter of Robert Ridgely. These children were by Mareen Duvall's first wife, whose name has never been discovered as he doubtless married her before leaving France.

He married for his second wife Susannah ———, whose identity is also a mystery. His children by this wife were Mareen, called the younger, who married Elizabeth Jacob, daughter of Capt. John Jacob;

Catherine, who married William Orrick, October 22, 1700; Mary, who married the Rev. Henry Hall, February 5, 1701; Elizabeth, who remained single; Johanna, who married Richard Poole, August 12, 1703, and Benjamin, who married Elizabeth Clarke, 1713.

* * *

Mareen Duvall, eldest son of the immigrant, married Frances Stockett and had by her a son Mareen, who married Sarah ———, and had a large family, of whom Mareen and Samuel were twins; born June 22, 1714. The latter was the father of John Pearçe Duvall, who was a lawyer and removed to Virginia and became a member of the Legislature there.

Western Branch Mareen Duvall, twin of Samuel, had among other children a daughter Kazia, who married Cornelius Duvall, a descendant of the younger Mareen, who removed to Kentucky and left a numerous progeny, one of whom was Judge Alvin Duvall of that state. Capt. John Duvall and Elizabeth Jones had twelve children. Elizabeth, the eldest, married Benjamin Warfield, youngest son of Richard Warfield, the pioneer of that name in Maryland, and was the ancestor of many distinguished men of Maryland by the name of Warfield, Dorsey, Ridgely, Griffith and Worthington.

Mary, the second daughter of Capt. John Duvall, married Edward Gaither, February 21, 1709, and had several children. Sarah, the third daughter, married Samuel Farmer, and left many children, among them Samuel, who served with reputation throughout the revolutionary war as an officer in the Maryland Line.

Lewis Duvall, son of Captain John, had a son William, who was an officer in the revolution. He married a Miss Johnson, Virginia, through whom Governor William P. Duvall, of Florida, and John Pope Duvall, of Richmond, descend.

Lewis Duvall's daughter Elizabeth married William Ridgely, grandson of Robert Ridgely, secretary to the council and afterward principal secretary of the province, ancestor of Hon. Charles Ridgely, Governor of Maryland.

Rachel, one of the daughters of Lewis Duvall, married Nathan Waters, whose son, Nathaniel Waters, married a daughter of the celebrated Mr. Rittenhouse, of Philadelphia. A daughter of Rachel Duvall Waters, married Richard Maccubbin, father of George Maccubbin, treasurer of Maryland, in 1827. Another of her daughters married Arthur Nelson, and was the mother of Dr. John Nelson, of the medical department of the Revolutionary Army, and of Gen. Roger Nelson, lawyer member of the Legislature and Congressman, and the grandmother of John Nelson, Attorney General of the United States and member of Congress.

* * *

Samuel Duvall and Elizabeth Clarke, who were married in the year 1687, had seven daughters and no sons. The eldest, Elizabeth, born October 6, 1697, married Edward Tyler, son of Robert and his wife, Susanna Duvall. Susanna Tyler (of Edward and Elizabeth) born February 24, 1717, married Benjamin Duvall, grandson of Mareen Duvall, the youngest son of the Huguenot, and had ten children, one of whom was Justice Gabrella Duvall. Another son, Benjamin, who married in 1772 Miss Jemima Taylor, was the ancestor of the late Isaac Harding Duvall, of West Virginia, a major general in the United States Army.

Susanna Duvall, who married Robert Tyler, Sr., had eight children one of whom, Robert Tyler, Jr., born August 9, 1704, married his first cousin and had five children, one of whom, Robert III, born November 5, 1727, married Miss Bradley, of Prince George County, Md., and had a son, Robert Bradley Tyler, and a

Rachel, one of the daughters of Lewis Duvall, married Nathan Waters, whose son, Nathaniel Waters, married a daughter of the celebrated Mr. Rittenhouse, of Philadelphia. A daughter of Rachel Duvall Waters, married Richard Mackubin, father of George Mackubin, treasurer of Maryland, in 1827. Another of her daughters married Arthur Nelson, and was the mother of Dr. John Nelson, of the medical department of the Revolutionary Army, and of Gen. Roger Nelson, former member of the Legislature and Congressman, and the grandmother of John Nelson, Attorney General of the United States and member of Congress.

* * *

Samuel Duvall and Elizabeth Clarke, who were married in the year 1697, had seven daughters and no sons. The eldest, Elizabeth, born October 6, 1697, married Edward Tyler, son of Robert and his wife, Susanna Duvall. Susanna Tyler (of Edward and Elizabeth) born February 24, 1717, married Benjamin Duvall, grandson of Mareen Duvall, the youngest son of the Huguenot, and had ten children, one of whom was Justice Gabriel Duvall. Another son, Benjamin, who married in 1772 Miss Jemima Taylor, was the ancestor of the late Isaac Harding Duvall, of West Virginia, a major general in the United States Army.

Susanna Duvall, who married Robert Tyler, Sr., had eight children one of whom, Robert Tyler, Jr., born August 2, 1704, married his first cousin and had five children, one of whom, Robert III, born November 1, 1727, married Miss Bradley, of Prince George's County, Md., and had a son, Robert Bradley Tyler, and a

daughter, Millicent. The son married first Miss Beans. After her death in 1757 he married secondly a daughter of Capt. Tobias Belt and had several children, of whom Dr. William Bradley Tyler, of Frederick City, Md., married Miss Murdock, and had several children.

* * *

Millicent, the daughter of Robert Tyler III, married De Colmore Beanes of Prince George County, Md., by whom she had a daughter, who married Mr. ——— Key (a son of Philip, a cousin of Francis Scott Key, the author of "The Star-Spangled Banner").

* * *

Lewis Duvall married March 5, 1699, Martha Ridgely, daughter of Robert Ridgely, principal secretary of the province, and had issue four daughters: the oldest Martha, lived with her father's stepmother, formerly the widow of Mareen Duvall, then the widow of Col. Henry Ridgely I, and finally the wife of Rev. Jacob Henderson. Martha Duvall was buried in the vault in the chapel with Mrs. Henderson. Her father is said to have removed to one of the Carolinas.

Mareen Duvall (the younger) was married October 2, 1701, to Elizabeth Jacobs (the daughter of Capt. John Jacobs, the first immigrant of that name to come to Maryland) and had issue eleven children; Mareen III, born November 14, 1702, married Ruth Howard and had fourteen children, one of whom, Mareen Howard Duvall, married Miss Wheeler, and among other children she had Howard Duvall, who married Mary, a daughter of Marsh Mareen Duvall, from whom descended Dr. Howard Mareen Duvall, of South River.

Elizabeth, a daughter of Mareen (the younger), married Dr. William Danune and had four daughters and one son; three daughters married three brothers by the name of Taylor—Samuel, Caleb and Richard.

* * *

Lewis Duvall married March 5, 1699, Martha Ridgely, daughter of Robert Ridgely, principal secretary of the province, and had issue four daughters: the oldest, Martha, lived with her father's stepmother, formerly the widow of Mareen Duvall, then the widow of Col. Henry Ridgely I, and finally the wife of Rev. Jacob Henderson. Martha Duvall was buried in the vault in the chapel with Mrs. Henderson. Her father is said to have removed to one of the Carolinas.

Mareen Duvall (the younger) was married October 1?, 1701, to Elizabeth Jacobs (the daughter of Capt. John Jacobs, the first immigrant of that name to come to Maryland) and had issue eleven children. Mareen III, born November 1?, 1702, married Ruth Howard and had fourteen children, one of whom, Mareen Howard Duvall, married Ann Wheeler, and among other children she had Howard Duvall, who married Mary, a daughter of March Mareen Duvall III, who is descended by Howard Mareen Duvall of Sandy Level.

Elizabeth, a daughter of Mareen the Immigrant, married Dr. William Williams and had two daughters and one son, three daughters, whose descendants bear the name of Ladler, Samuel, Grafton and Howard.

Martha, one of the daughters of Samuel Taylor, married Joseph Cross, by whom she had seven children. The eldest son was an officer in the United States Navy; had two others, Howerton and Freeman, who were officers in the war of 1812.

Samuel Duvall, son of Mareen (the younger) born November 27, 1707, married May 16, 1732, Elizabeth Mullikin, born September 25, 1717, daughter of James Mullikin, who came to Maryland in 1660. They had issue, ten children.

One of their sons, Samuel Duvall, born July 9, 1740, married Mary Higgins and had ten children. He was quartermaster of the Revolutionary Army.

* * *

Samuel Duvall and Mary Higgins Duvall, his wife, also had ten children, among them Tobias, Barton and Beale.

Tobias married Miss Willett and had several children.

Among Tobias' grandsons are Rev. Frederick Beale Duvall, of the Presbyterian church, and William A. Duvall, of Baltimore, his brother, and their cousin, the late Ferdinand Duvall, a captain in the Confederate Army.

* * *

Samuel and Joseph Duvall, sons of Daniel of Tobias, and Dr. Philip Barton Duvall and Samuel F. Duvall, sons of the late Richard I. Duvall, and Thomas Mitchell were other grandsons of Tobias and were all soldiers in the Confederate Army. Samuel and Joseph, sons of Daniel, were killed in battle, and Dr. Philip Barton Duvall was killed on the battlefield at Chancellorsville, Va.

Samuel and Mary Duvall also had a son Barton, who married Hannah Isaacs, daughter of Richard Isaacs, Jr., and Nancy Williams, and had four sons—Richard Isaacs, Dr. Barton, Samuel and Dr. Joseph Isaacs Duvall.

[illegible] children. He was quartermaster of the Revolutionary Army.

* * *

Samuel Duvall and Mary Hughes Duvall, his wife, also had ten children, among them Tobias, Reuben and Reese.

Tobias married Miss Waller and had seven children.

Among Tobias' grandsons are Rev. Frederick Rolle Duvall of the Presbyterian Church, and William A. Duvall of Baltimore, his brother, and their cousin, the late Ferdinand Duvall, a captain in the Confederate Army.

* * *

Samuel and Joseph Duvall, sons of Daniel of Tobias, and the Philip Barton Duvall and [illegible] Duvall, sons of Captain Richard I. Duvall, and Thomas Mackall, were great-grandsons of Tobias and were all soldiers in the Confederate Army. Samuel and Joseph, sons of Daniel, were killed in battle, and D. Philip Barton Duvall was [illegible] and buried at [illegible]sonville, Va.

Samuel and Mary Duvall also had a son Burton, who married Hannah James, daughter of Richard James, Jr.

Richard Isaacs Duvall was a member of the Maryland Legislature and Register of Wills. He married first his cousin, Sarah A. Duvall, daughter of Tobias, by whom he had Dr. Philip Barton Duvall and Samuel Duvall and several other children; and, secondly, he married Rachael M. Waring, a daughter of Francis and Elizabeth Waring, by whom he had several children, one of whom is Richard Warren Duvall, a well-known and prominent member of the Baltimore bar, who married Nannie Webster Goldsborough, daughter of Dr. John Schley Goldsborough, of Frederick, Md., lineal descendant of Hon. Robert Goldsborough and Elizabeth Greenberry, daughter of Col. Nicholas Greenberry.

Samuel Duvall, son of Barton, lived and died in Washington, D. C. He left several children, among them Nelson Duvall and Mrs. Brecht and Mrs. Simpson.

Dr. Joseph I. Duvall, son of Barton, married Mary A. Mitchell, and died in 1883, leaving now surviving him one son. Dr. John M. Duvall, of Prince George County, Md.

Dr. Philip Barton Duvall, son of Barton, died about 1850, and has only one child surviving—Mrs. Patty.

Beale Duvall, son of Samuel and Mary Higgins Duvall, married twice—first, Miss Belt, daughter of Jeremiah Belt, and had one daughter, who married a Mr. Walker; second, Miss Williams, and had seven children, one of whom, John, married Eliza Ridgely, a descendant of Governor Ridgely and of John Eager Howard, also a Governor of Maryland. From John and Eliza Ridgely Duvall are descended Mrs. Benjamin Price, of New York; Howards, Posts, Whelans, and others, of Baltimore, and Mr. Charles E. Fendall, a member of the Baltimore bar.

* * *

John Duvall, a son of Mareen Duvall, the younger, born February 20, 1712–13, married in 1737 Ann Fowler and had seven children. Their oldest daughter, Elizabeth married December 4, 1759 John Macgill, a son of Rev. James Macgill. Their eldest son, Marsh Mareen Duvall, born April 17, 1741, was an officer during the revolutionary war. He married in 1762 Sarah Hall, a granddaughter of Rev. Henry Hall, of St. James' parish, and Mary Duvall his wife, a daughter of Mareen Duvall, the Huguenot.

John Duvall, the son of Marsh Mareen, born June 28, 1763, married November 28, 1798, Rebecca Rawlings, a near relative of Col. Moses Rawlings, of the revolutionary army, and their son, the late John Rawlings Duvall, of Baltimore, born November 28, 1811, married October 17, 1837, Elizabeth Reiman; was the father of H. Reiman Duvall, of New York (formerly president of the F. C. & P. Railroad Company, who married Nannie Gordon Thomas, daughter of the late Dr. John Hanson Thomas, of Baltimore) and of Mary Rebecca Duvall and John R. Duvall, of Baltimore.

In November, 1774, at a meeting in Upper Marlboro, Prince George County, Marsh Mareen Duvall was appointed on a committee of freeman "to carry into execution within the said county the Association of the Congress."

It is interesting to the genealogist to note how names are changed and misspelled in ancient documents and records. The old Huguenot's Christian name was certainly, in French, Marin, and the Rev. Mr. Charles W. Baird, the Huguenot historian, accepts the spelling of the name as Marin, and writes that the origin of the name Duvall was probably in Lorraine from La Ville Remirement.

[illegible]

[illegible] relative of Col. Moses Rawlings, of the revolutionary army, and their son, the late John Rawlings Duvall of Baltimore, born November 22, 1822, married October 15, 1847, Elizabeth Ramsay; was the father of H. Rieman Duvall of New York (formerly president of the [illegible] Railroad Company, who married Nannie Gordon Thomas, daughter of the late Dr. John Hanson Thomas, of Baltimore), and of Mary Rebecca Duvall and John R. Duvall, of Baltimore.

In November, 1774, at a meeting in Upper Marlboro, Prince George's County, Mareen Duvall was appointed on a committee of [illegible] "to carry into execution within the said county the Association of the Congress."

It is interesting to the genealogist to note how names are changed and misspelled in ancient documents and records. The old Huguenot's Christian name was certainly, in French, Marin, and the Rev. Mr. Charles W. Baird, the Huguenot historian, accepts the spelling of the name as Marine and writes that the origin of the name Duvall was probably in Lorraine from La Ville Romaine.

HOLY TRINITY CHURCH, Near Collington, Maryland

The Society of Mareen Duvall Descendants and the Pilgrimage to the Church he founded at Collington, Maryland

By MARY V. DUVALL

ON February 22nd, 1926, a meeting was held at Baltimore, Maryland by the Descendants of Mareen Duvall, its object being to gather into a Society the progeny of the French Huguenot, in order to perpetuate his memory and deeds, as well as those of worthy descendants.

A Constitution and By-laws was adopted, officers elected and the name chosen was, "SOCIETY OF MAREEN DUVALL DESCENDANTS." It was further arranged that on Sunday, July 24th, 1927, the society consisting of those already enrolled as members, would make a pilgrimage to Collington, Prince George's County, Maryland, in order to attend the services at Holy Trinity, the little Episcopal church, built over two hundred years ago, by one who renounced his home and country for the sake of religious freedom.

The history of that time tells us, that "as early as the year 1648, Ceciluis Calvert instructed Governor Stone,

to give to any Frenchman who was settled, or who might hereafter settle in the Colony, all the rights and privileges enjoyed by the English and Irish emigrants, who alone up to that time enjoyed the rights of citizenship."

Among the earliest and most prominent of the French Huguenots was Mareen Duvall, who arrived in Maryland early in 1659 and on August 28th, 1659, a tract of land on the south side of South River in Anne Arundel County, near the site of New London, was surveyed and patented to him under the name of "La Val," in memory of the family estates in France. He was a young man at the time of his arrival, and by the acquisition of other large tracts of land the enterprising young emigrant soon became one of the largest gentlemen planters of South River, and an important merchant of New London Town. He became identified with the most influential men of Maryland, and by an Act of the Assembly, was appointed one of the Commissioners to lay off and survey ports of entry to the County, and his services during an Indian outbreak in 1683 was recognized and highly rewarded. His property included several thousand acres in Anne Arundel and Prince George's counties where he lived the easy life of a country gentleman.

That this provident French refugee was of the Protestant faith is evident from the fact that he built at his own expense on his home plantation in Prince George's County, a chapel for private worship. In 1705 his son John deeded the land on which the chapel stood to Queen Anne for the use of the parish, but it was not until 1741 that it became a parish church, supported by the Community, for up to that time it was maintained solely by the Duvall family.

to give to any Frenchman who was [illegible] might hereafter settle in the Colony [illegible] privileges enjoyed by the English and [illegible] who alone up to that time enjoyed the [illegible] ship."

Among the earliest and most prominent [illegible] Huguenots was Mareen Duvall, who arrived [illegible] early in 1659 and on August 28th, 16[illegible] on the south side of South River in Anne [illegible] near the site of New London, was surveyed [illegible] to him under the name of "La Val," [illegible] family estates in France. He was a [illegible] time of his arrival, and by the acquisition [illegible] tracts of land the enterprising young [illegible] became one of the largest gentlemen [illegible] River, and an important merchant of [illegible] He became identified with the most [illegible] Maryland, and by an Act of the Assembly [illegible] one of the Commissioners to lay off [illegible] entry to the County, and his services [illegible] outbreak in 1683 was recognized and [illegible] His property included, several thousand [illegible] Arundel and Prince George's counties [illegible] easy life of a country gentleman."

That this provident French [illegible] Protestant faith is evident from the [illegible] at his own expense on his home plantation [illegible] George's County, a chapel for private [illegible] 1705 his son John deeded the land on [illegible] stood to Queen Anne for the use of [illegible] was not until 1741 that it became [illegible] supported by the Community, for up [illegible] was maintained solely by the Duvall family.

The annals of the Duvall family is of great interest to many people in America, for nearly every State in the Union has among its best citizens descendants of Mareen Duvall, and almost every prominent family in Maryland has the blood of the Huguenot in its veins. Among them may be mentioned, William P. Duvall, first Territorial Governor of Florida, Governor Francis Thomas of Maryland, the late Isaac Harding Duvall, Major General of the United States Army, Judge Alvin Duvall of Kentucky, Governor English of Indiana, Major Wm. Penn Duvall of the United States Army, Judge Gabriel Duvall, grandson of the Huguenot, who was Associate Justice of the Supreme Court from 1811 to 1836, at the time when the gifted Judge John Marshall was at the helm. Justice Gabriel Duvall was the historian of the family, and at his death in 1840 many of the unwritten traditions of the family on which he was well informed, passed away, and with the disastrous fire of Old Hall in Prince George's County, many papers together with original portraits and relics were destroyed.

It is interesting to note that Mareen Duvall was married three times. By two of these wives he had six children. His third wife, however, did not have any children. She was the charming Mary Staunton, who after his death became the wife of Col. Henry Ridgely, who with her, administered upon Mareen Duvall's estate. She survived Col. Ridgely and was made his executrix. He left her the bulk of his estates, which included his home plantation "Cotton," "Mary's Delight," "Larkin's Folly," "Hogg Neck," three hundred acres of Ridgely's Lot at Huntington, 500 acres of Wardridge, Larkins Forrest, and the remaining part of his estates in England. She became the wife of Rev. Jacob Henderson, Commissary of the Province, and the

The annals of the Duvall family is of great
to many people in America, for nearly every
the Union has among its best citizens descen
Mareen Duvall, and almost every prominent f
Maryland has the blood of the Huguenot in i
Among them may be mentioned, William P.
first Territorial Governor of Florida, Governor
Thomas of Maryland, the late Isaac Harding
Major General of the United States Army, Judg
Duval of Kentucky, Governor English of
Major Wm. Penn Duvall of the United States
Judge Gabriel Duvall, grandson of the Huguenot
was Associate Justice of the Supreme Court fr
to 1836, at the time when the gifted Judge John M
was at the helm. Justice Gabriel Duvall
historian of the family, and at his death in 1840
the unwritten traditions of the family on which
well informed, passed away, and with the destruct
of Old Hall in Prince George's County, many
together with original portraits and relics were de

It is interesting to note that Mareen Duv
married three times. By two of these wives he
children. His third wife, however, did not hav
children. She was the charming Mary Staunton, w
after his death became the wife of Col. Henry R
who with her, administered upon Mareen D
estate. She survived Col. Ridgely and was it
executrix. He left her the bulk of his estate,
included his home plantation, "Cotton,"
Doughs," "Larkin's Folly," "Hogg Neck" an
dred acres of Ridgely's Lot at Huntington, 300
Warfridge, Larkins Forrest, and the remaining
his estates in England. She became the wife
Jacob Henderson, Commissary of the Province,

first Rector of Holy Trinity Church. He was sent by the Bishop of London to report on the state of the Anglican church in Maryland, and served as the Rector of Queen Anne Parish from 1717 until 1751.

Rev. Mr. Henderson and his wife applied themselves and their ample fortunes to the decoration and adornment of his church, and the repairs for some time were made at their expense. They lived at Belair, the beautiful Duvall estate, which afterwards became the home of Governor Ogle and is now the property of Mr. James Woodward of New York.

Soon after Mr. Henderson took charge of Holy Trinity, he was commissioned by the Vestry to expend fifty pounds on the purchase of a velvet cushion with gold tassels, a velvet pulpit-cloth edged with gold, a purple velvet alter cloth and a marble baptismal font. Later the records show, that more funds were used to purchase a heavy beaten silver Communion service with the Tower hallmark, which was brought from London in 1718 and which it is said is still in use. Prof. Hart says in his account that in 1720, the vestry gave Mr. Henderson authority to commission the pioneer Artist, Gustavus Hesselius of Sweden to decorate the unpainted woodwork of the church, the alterpiece and Communion Table. A year later Hesselius agreed to begin a large painting of "The Last Supper," to hang in the space above the alterpiece. It was not until 1725 that the painting was finished and placed in position, for which the artist was paid seventeen pounds. It was said to be the first work of art commissioned for a building in America. Later this painting mysteriously disappeared. Whether it was taken away for safe keeping while the church was undergoing repairs, or was spirited away later in the confusion of the times, no one has ever been

[illegible]

[illegible]

[illegible] in 1718 and which is said to fit [illegible]

[illegible] It was not until 1695 that the [illegible] had been painted in addition, for when [illegible] be the first work of a [illegible] in America. [illegible] Whether it was [illegible] church was [illegible] repairs, [illegible]

able to say, but this painting lost over two hundred years ago would be a valued treasure, if the mystery of its disappearance could be solved and the painting located.

A large window occupies the space, and memorial windows perpetuate the memory of the Duvall, Mullikin, Bowie and other old families of Anne Arundel and Prince George's Counties.

The Rev. Mr. Henderson died in 1751 and several ministers succeeded him. Everything went smoothly it seems in the parish until about 1772 when Mr. Boucher took charge. He was an Englishman and was of course bound by an oath of allegiance to the King. His loyalty was not relished by his patriotic congregation, and one Sunday in 1775 he was warned by letter that if he read the same prayer he used for the Royal family he would be shot in the chancel. But he went to church, robed himself, and walked courageously down the aisle to the reading desk, a pistol in each hand, and proceeded to read the forbidden prayer. For some time it is said, he preached his sermons with a loaded pistol lying beside his prayer book. Later when an excited crowd of patriots gathered before the church door, one of the vestrymen, father of Governor Sprigg, went to Boucher and told him that he would not be allowed to preach, but the undaunted minister holding his sermon in one hand and a pistol in the other, exclaimed, "you can only prevent my entrance by taking my life." The Patriots really did not wish to harm him, but they did not intend to have a parson who still proclaimed openly "God save the King." When the last ship left Annapolis for England, Boucher and his wife were on it, never to return. His property, which was considerable, was confiscated and sold, but he never lost his interest in

[illegible]

[illegible]

[illegible]

Holy Trinity Church, for after the Revolution he wrote to friends in terms that showed all bitterness had passed away.

So here under the lofty trees that have shaded the quaint little church for so many years, the descendants of Mareen Duvall will gather to honor and venerate the character and patriotism of the founder and patron of Holy Trinity Church and their progenitor.

Last Will and Testament of Mareen Duvall · 1694

IN THE NAME OF GOD AMEN I Mareen Duvall of the County of Ann Arundell in the Province of Maryland Merchant whom am at this present of good and perfect memory but weak in body at this time praised be God and knowing the uncertainty of this mortall life am willing for the future peace and quietness of all or any person or persons herein concerned to settle that estate which it hath pleased the Almighty to bless me with all by this my last Will and Testament in manner and form following.

Imprs. First I bequeath my Soul into the hands of Almighty God the donor of it and my body to be interred in the ground from whence it was taken and at the discretion of my Exec'x hereafter named in sure and certain hope of the resurrection to eternall life through our Lord Jesus Christ.

Item. I give and bequeath unto my well beloved wife Mary Duvall this plantation whereon I now dwell dureing her naturall life without any trouble or molestation of either of my sons or daughters or any other person or persons herein mentioned for them and on their behalf this said plantation being and appertaining to the one moyety of six hundred acres called The Middle Plantation and that my said wife shall and may such use and benefit of the other moyety of land appertaining to this tract with the plantation thereof as shall seem good unto her or as she shall have occasion for timbers and

Last Will

Mareen 694

IN THE NAME OF

the Houses of

land Merchant whom

perfect memory but

be God and knowing

are ordained for the

any person or persons

estate which it hath

with all by this my last

Law form following

other necessarys for buildings houses and repairations of buildings of houses cask or the like or any other necessarys without waste or impreachment of the same and not other wise dureing her naturall life.

Item. I give and bequeath unto my son Lewis Duvall all that my three hundred acres of land and plantation whereon my eldest son Mareen Duvall now dwelleth it being a moyety lying on the South East part or end of six hundred acres of land called The Middle Plantation and situate in the County of Ann Arundell afsd to have and to hold the said plantation and to the heirs of his body lawfully begotten forever and for want of such issue then my will is that the same be and go to the next heir or heiress by and from me lawfully and lineally descended.

Item. I give Grant and bequeath to my son Lewis Duvall my now dwelling plantation after the decease of loveing wife Mary Duvall with the three hundred acres of land whereon the same is situated it being the other moyety of the aforesaid six hundred acres of land called The Middle Plantation situate in the County of Ann Arundell aforesaid to have and to hold the said plantation and moyety viz: The three hundred acres of land besides the plantation and tract unto him my said son Lewis Duvall and to the heirs of his body lawfully begotten forever and in case of default of such issue then to descend to the next heir or heiress by and from me lawfully and lineally descended.

Item. I give grant and bequeath unto my daughter Elizab' Duvall that three hundred seventy and five acres of land called and known by the name of Bowdels Choice Lying situate in the County of Calvert and adjoining to a place called by the name of Boares Creek to have and to hold the same unto her and the heirs of her body lawfully born and begotten forever and in case

other necessary for building houses and repairations of buildings of house cask or the like or any other necessary without waste or impeachment of the same and not other. She devising her natural life.

Item. I give and bequeath unto my son Lewis Duvall all that my three hundred acres of land and plantation whereon my eldest son Mareen Duvall now dwelleth it being a moyety lying on the South East part and of six hundred acres of land called The Middle Plantation and situate in the County of Ann Arundell and to have and to hold the said plantation and to the heirs of his body lawfully begotten forever and for want of such issue then my will is that the same be and go to the next heir or heires by and from me lawfully and legally descended.

Item. I give Grant and bequeath to my son Lewis Duvall my now dwelling plantation after the decease of my loving wife Mary Duvall with the three hundred acres of land whereon the same is situated it being the other moyety of the aforesaid six hundred acres of land called The Middle Plantation situate in the County of Ann Arundel aforesaid to have and to hold the said plantation and moyety viz. The three hundred acres of land besides the plantation and tract unto him my said son Lewis Duvall and to the heirs of his body lawfully begotten forever and in case of default of such issue then to descend to the next heir or heires by and from me lawfully and legally descended.

Item. I give grant and bequeath unto my daughter Eliza Duvall that three hundred seventy and five acres of land called and known by the name of Bowdels Choice lying and being in the County of Calvert and adjoining to a place called by the name of Bowles Creek to have and to hold the same unto her and the heirs of her body lawfully born and begotten forever and in case

of default of such issue then to be and to go to the next heir or heiress of from and by me lawfully and lineally descended.

Item. I give and bequeath unto my son Benjamin Duvall two hundred acres of land it being a moyety or one half part of four hundred acres of land called and known by the name of Howertons Range lying situate and being in the County of Calvert aforesaid and that part or moyety that lyeth on the South side of the said four hundred acres it being equally divided to have and to hold the same unto him my said son Benjamin and to the heirs of his body lawfully begotten forever and in default of such issue then my will is that the same said moyety or part shall fall or go to the next heir or heiress of or from me legally descended.

Item. I give and bequeath to my daughter Katherine Duvall two hundred acres of land it being the other half or moyety of that four hundred acres aforesaid called Howertons Range and that half or moyety lying on the North Part or side thereof to have and to hold the same unto her my said daughter Katherine and unto the heirs on her body lawfully begotten and born forever, and in default of such issue then my will is that the same part or moyety be and go unto the next heir or heiress of by or from me lineally descended.

Item. I give grant and bequeath unto my son Mareen Duvall the younger born unto me by my late wife Susanna all that my three hundred acres of land called The Plains lying in Calvert County aforesaid to have and to hold the same unto him my said son Mareen the younger as aforesaid and to the heirs of his body lawfully begotten forever and in default of such issue then my will is that the same return to the next heir or heiress of by and from me lawfully and lineally descended.

Item. I give grant and bequeath unto my daughter

Mary Duvall all that my three hundred and twenty acres of land and plantation called and known by the name of Morleys Grove lying situate in the County of Ann Arundell and also three hundred acres of land called Marleys Lott lying in the said County of Ann Arundell to have and to hold the same said two tracts containing six hundred and seventy acres of land to her my said daughter Mary Duvall and the heirs of her body lawfully begotten and born forever and for default of such issue then it is my will that the same be and go to the next heir or heiress of by or from me lawfully or lineally descended.

Item. I give grant and bequeath unto my youngest daughter Johanna Duvall all that my three hundred and eleven acres of land called and known by the name of Larkins Choice lying and being in the County of Ann Arundell aforesaid to have and to hold the same unto her my said daughter Johanna and to the heirs of her body lawfully born and begotten forever and for want of such issue then my will is that the same be go and return to the next heir or heiress of from or by me lawfully and lineally descended.

Item. It is my will and desire if my youngest child or children should dye without such heirs or heiress as before nominated and exprest so that there will be non under them to succeed and possess the said lands by me bequeathed then in case of default of such issue to fall and go to by descent then my will is and desire that such and so many of them if any should dye as aforesaid that then their said land shall asend and go back to the first heir or heiress at law and so to be and remain to the rightfull heirs and heiresses from and so descended as aforesaid to the longest liver of my posterity.

Item. It is my will and desire that my said children before mentioned be and remain with my wife that now

is dureing their minorities and it is my further will that my sons be free and of capacity to work for themselves when they come to the age of eighteen years and my daughters at the age of sixteen years not questioning but that my said wife will be loveing and tender unto them and I do hereby conjoin her to use her endeavour to educate them in that fear of God and obedience to man.

Item. I give and grant unto my daughter Johanna that two hundred acres of land called Duvalls Range lying situate in County of Ann Arundel aforesaid to have and to hold the same unto her the said Johanna and the heirs of her body begotten forever and in case of default of such issue then to return and asend to the heir male next unto her and preceeding her and in default of such heirs then to asend to the heires or heiress next lawfully descended from me.

Item. I give grant and bequeath unto my son John Duvall five shillings Sterling money of England to be paid unto him after my decease by my Executrix hereafter named.

Item. I give and bequeath unto my daughter Elizabeth Roberts the wife of John Roberts five shillings Sterling money of England to be paid unto her after my deseace by my Executrix hereafter named.

Item. I give and bequeath unto my son Samuel Duvall five shillings Sterling to be paid by my Executrix as aforesaid unto him after my decease.

Item. I give and bequeath to my daughter Elizabeth Duvall one hundred and fifty pounds Sterling money of England to be paid her by my Executrix hereafter named after my decease when she shall come to the age of sixteen years or day of marriage which shall first happen.

Item. I give and bequeath to my son Mareen Duvall the eldest of that name five shillings Sterling money of

in debarring them [illegible] and it is my
my wife by [illegible] and of capacity to [illegible]
when they come to the age of eighte[en]
daughters at the age of sixteen years
not that my said wife will be loving [illegible]
ment and I do hereby enjoin her to [illegible]
educate them in that fear of God and [illegible]

Item. I give and grant unto my daug[hter]
that two hundred acres of land called [illegible]
lying situate in County of Ann Arund[el]
have and to hold the same unto her [illegible]
and the heirs of her body begotten for[ever]
of default of such issue than to return [illegible]
heir male next unto her and proceeding [illegible]
of such heirs then to ascend to the heires
lawfully descended from me.

Item. I give grant and bequeath un[to]
Darall five shillings Sterling money of
paid unto him after my decease by my
after named.

Item. I give and bequeath unto
Elizabeth Roberts the wife of John Rob[erts]
Sterling money of England to be paid
my decease by my Executrix hereafter n[amed]

Item. I give and bequeath unto [illegible]
Darall five shillings Sterling to be paid [illegible]
as aforesaid unto him after my decease.

Item. I give and bequeath to my dau[ghter]
Darall one hundred and fifty pounds
of England to be paid her by my Exe[cutrix]
married after my decease when she shall
of sixteen years or day of marriage [illegible]
happen.

Item. I give and bequeath to my son
the eldest of that name five shillings S[terling]

England to be paid unto him by my Executrix hereafter named after my decease.

Item. I give and bequeath unto my daughter Johanna Duvall one hundred and fifty pounds Sterling money of England to be paid unto her by my Executrix after my decease when she shall come to the age of sixteen years or day of marriage which shall first happen.

Item. I give and bequeath to my daughter Mary Duvall one hundred and fifty pounds Sterling money of England to be paid by my Executrix unto her after my decease when she shall come to the age of sixteen years or at the day of marriage.

Item. I give unto my daughter Katherine Duvall one hundred and fifty pounds Sterling money of England to be paid unto her by my Executrix after my decease when she shall come to the age of sixteen years or day of marriage which shall first happen.

Item. I give and bequeath unto my son Mareen Duvall the younger son of my late wife Susannah one hundred and fifty pounds of good lawful money of England to be paid unto him after my decease by my Executrix hereafter named when he shall come to be at the age of one and twenty years.

Item. I give and bequeath to my son Benjamin Duvall one hundred and fifty pounds Sterling money of England to be paid unto him after my decease by my Executrix as hereafter shall be named when he shall come to the age of one and twenty years.

Item. I give and bequeath to my son Lewis Duvall one hundred and fifty pounds good and lawful moneys of England to be paid unto him by my Executrix when he shall come to the age of one and twenty years after my decease.

Item. It is my will and desire that if any of my sons or daughters should decease in the interval before they

England to be paid unto him by my Executrix hereafter named after my decease.

Item. I give and bequeath unto my daughter Johanna Dowell one hundred and fifty pounds sterling money of England to be paid unto her by my Executrix after my decease when she shall come to the age of sixteen years or day of marriage which shall first happen.

Item. I give and bequeath to my daughter [illegible] Dowell one hundred and fifty pounds Sterling money of England to be paid by my Executrix unto her after my decease when she shall come to the age of sixteen years or at the day of marriage.

Item. I give unto my daughter Katharine Dowell one hundred and fifty pounds Sterling money of England to be paid unto her by my Executrix after my decease when she shall come to the age of sixteen years or day of marriage which shall first happen.

Item. I give and bequeath unto my son Marvin Dowell the younger son of my late wife Susannah one hundred and fifty pounds of good lawful money of England to be paid unto him after my decease by my Executrix hereafter named when he shall come to the age of one and twenty years.

Item. I give and bequeath to my son Benjamin Dowell one hundred and fifty pounds sterling money of England to be paid unto him after my decease by my Executrix as hereafter shall be named when he shall come to the age of one and twenty years.

Item. I give and bequeath to my son Lewis Dowell one hundred and fifty pounds good and lawful money of England to be paid unto him by my Executrix when he shall come to the age of one and twenty years after my decease.

Item. It is my will and desire that if any of my sons or daughters should decease in the interval before [illegible]

come to their full age herein specified that then their part or portions being one hundred and fifty pounds Sterling be equally divided and given to the survivors by equal portion to say amongst my sons and daughters herein concerned viz; that one hundred and fifty pounds each.

Item. I give and bequeath to my son John Duvall all my wearing apparel and my silver tobacco box to be given unto him by my Executrix after my decease.

Item. It is my desire that all and whatsoever debts I owe to any person whomsoever in right or conscience and *preperty* be paid by my Executrix hereafter named.

Last I do make constitute ordain and appoint my trusty and well beloved wife Mary Duvall to be my whole and sole Executrix of this my last Will and Testament and in case of mortality or death then it is my will to constitute and appoint my son beloved son John Duvall and my aforesaid son Lewis and my son in law Robert Tyler to be my so executors to act and do according to the office of executors for the good wellfair and benefit of my said children.

Item. I do nominate constitute and appoint that according to my earnest desire and request my trusty and well beloved children and supervisors as well as co executors in case of my wifes mortality will see all this my will and testament duely and truly performed according to the true intent and meaning of it.

And Lastly all former wills and Testaments either orall or written I do by these presents make null and void and of no effect and do ratifie and confirm this my last Will and Testament and do so publish and declare the same in the presence of the witnessess hereafter named and for a testimony hereof I have hereunto sett my hand and seal this second day of August Annoq Dom 1694.

come to their full age herein specified the
part or portions being one hundred and
Sterling be equally divided and given to
by equal portion to say amongst my sons
lawson concerned viz that one hundred and
each.

Item. I give and bequeath to my son
all my wearing apparel and my silver tobac
given unto him by my Executrix after

Item. It is my desire that all and what
I owe to any person whomsoever in right
and property be paid by my Executrix here

Last I do make constitute ordain and
trusty and well beloved wife Mary Duval
whole and sole Executrix of this my la
Testament and in case of mortality or dea
my will to constitute and appoint my son
John Duvall and my aforesaid son Lewis
law Robert Tyler to be my so executors to
according to the office of executor for the
and benefit of my said children.

Item. I do nominate constitute and
according to my earnest desire and request
and well beloved children and supervisors
so executors in case of my wifes mortality
this my will and testament duely and tru
according to the true intent and meaning o

And Lastly all former wills and Testa
orall or entered I do by these presents make
and of no effect and do ratifie and confir
last Will and Testament and do so publish
the same in the presence of the witnesses
named and for a testimony hereof I have
my hand and seal this second day of August
1734.

Memorand: that I give and bequeath to my daughter Susanna one silver tankard to be given by my Executrix after my decease.

Item. And further my will is that if any of those my heires as before nomonated shall inter marry with any particular person without the knowledge and advice or consent of these my Executors or Executrix as above mentioned that then it shall be left to the discretion of my Executrix or Executors as before mentioned whether to assist them with the aforesaid moneys that is bequeathed and granted to them by this my last Will and Testament and if so be that it shall please this my Executrix and beloved wife Mary Duvall to refuse the management of this my last Will and Testament then she is quietly to possess and enjoy the thirds of my estate and the entire acre and management of the rest of my estate to remain in the breasts of my Executors as above named to see that this my last will and desire be duly and truely executed and performed.

In testimony whereof I have sett to my hand and sealed it with my seal the day and year first above written.

Mareen Duvall (Seal)

This was published and declared to be the last Will and Testament of Mareen Duvall, Merchant in manner and form as above before us *Testes: William Rpoer—William Goodman—Richard Cheser—Jervis Morgan—Clement Davis.

Under the foregoing Will was subscribed thus viz: This will in common form proved this 13th August, 1694, before me

Henry Boyle—Dep'ty Comm'sy.

Recorded in Liber No. 2 folio 327 &c., in the Land Office of Maryland, Annapolis, Maryland.

[illegible] *Moreover*, that I give and bequeath to [illegible] Susanna one silver tankard to be given by [illegible] after my decease.

[illegible] *Item.* And further my will is that if any [illegible] before as before enumerated shall inter marr[illegible] particular person without the knowledge an[illegible] consent of these my Executors or Executr[illegible] mentioned that then it shall be left to the [illegible] my Executrix or Executors as before mentio[illegible] to assist them with the aforesaid moneys [illegible] bequeathed and granted to them by this my L[illegible] Testament and if so be that it shall ple[illegible] Executrix and beloved wife Mary Duvall [illegible] management of this my last Will and Testa[illegible] she is quietly to possess and enjoy the [illegible] estate and the entire care and management [illegible] of my estate to remain in the breasts of my [illegible] above named to see that this my last will [illegible] be duly and truly executed and performed [illegible]

[illegible] In testimony whereof I have set to m[illegible] sealed it with my seal the day and year [illegible] written.

[illegible] Mareen D[illegible]

[illegible] This was published and declared to be [illegible] and Testament of Mareen Duvall, Merchant [illegible] and form as above before us "Testes: William [illegible] William Goodman—Richard Clarke—Jerv[illegible] Clement Davis.

[illegible]

GENERATION

1st *MAREEN DUVA
b. Normandy, Franc
d. Maryland, Aug. 1

2nd [1][2]BENJAMIN m. [17
b. abt. 1683

3rd [1]WILLIAM m. [1745]
b. 1723
d. 1810
of Prince George's Co.
moved to Frederick C

4th [2]†WILLIAM m. [abt
b. 1750
d. 1825
of Frederick Co.

5th [1]JOHN PRATHER m.
b. 1777
d. 1823
of Frederick Co.

6th [1]WILLIAM TYLER
b. 1814
d. 1865

7th

1 ‡W
2 Ed
3 Joh
4 Fra
5 Ma
6 Zer
7 Sec
8 Cha
9 Ka

Note.—Compiled and printed in 1902.

†William Duvall commanded the ba
††Dr. Grafton Duvall was born 178
*Daniel Duvall was an officer (Color
‡William Caywood Duvall is cashier

Memorand. that I give and bequeath to m
Susanna one silver tankard to be given by my
after my decease.

Item. And further my will is that if any o
hereof as before enumerated shall inter marr
particular person without the knowledge and
consent of these my Executors or Executri
mentioned that then it shall be left to the d
my Executrix or Executors as before mention
to assist them with the aforesaid moneys
mentioned and granted to them by this my la
Testament and if so be that it shall plea
Executrix and beloved wife Mary Duvall co
management of this my last Will and Testa
she is quietly to possess and enjoy the ch
estate and the entire acre and management
of my estate to remain in the breasts of my E
above named to see that this my last will
be duly and truly executed and performed.

In testimony whereof I have set to my
sealed it with my seal the day and year
written.

Mareen Du

This was published and declared to be th
and Testament of Mareen Duvall, Merchant
and form as above before us "Teste: William
William Goodman—Richard Cheese—Jervis
Clement Davis.

Under the foregoing Will was subscribed
This will in common form proved this 13
1694, before me

Henry Boyle—Dep'ty C

Recorded in Liber No. 2 folio 327 &c., in
Office of Maryland, Annapolis, Maryland.

Partial Genealogy of the Duvall Family in Maryland

GENERATION

1st

MAREEN DUVALL, m. { 1st ———— / 2nd Susanna ———— / 3rd Mary Stanton }
b. Normandy, France,—— d. Maryland, Aug. 1694.

Note.—In 1659 Mareen Duvall, "the Huguenot," received a grant of land on the south side of South River, in Anne Arundel Co. The church and other provincial records show that he became a prominent, useful and trusted member of the community in which he chose his home. He was a large landowner, planter and merchant, and was a man of liberal education for the times. The genealogy of his family has been traced back into the eighth century. The old "Chateau de La Val," commenced in the ninth century, is still standing in Normandy. Mareen named his homestead on South River "La Val," after the family estates in France.

2nd

[12]BENJAMIN m. [1713] Sophia Griffith
b. abt. 1683 | b. Apr. 27, 1691, Daughter of William and Sarah [Maccubbin] Griffith

1 Mareen m. Frances Stockett
2 John m. Elizabeth Jones
3 Eleanor m. John Roberts [of Va.]
4 Samuel m. [1687] Elizabeth Clarke
5 Susanna m. Robert Tyler
6 Lewis m. [1699] Martha Ridgely
7 Mareen m. [1701] Elizabeth Jacobs [the younger]
8 Catherine m. [1700] Wm. Orrick
9 Mary m. [1701] Rev. Henry Hall
10 Elizabeth
11 Johanna m. [1703] Richard Poole

Note.—Susanna and Robert Tyler were ancestors of President Tyler.

Note.—A daughter of Lewis and Martha (Ridgely) Duvall was the mother of Dr. John Nelson, of the Revolutionary Army, and of Gen. Roger Nelson, and grandmother of John Nelson, Attorney-General of the U. S.

3rd

[3]WILLIAM m. [1743] Priscilla Pannell
b. 1723, d. 1810, of Prince George's Co. moved to Frederick Co. | b. 1727, d. 1798, of Prince George's Co.

Note.—Lewis Duvall, son of Capt. John and Elizabeth Jones, was the ancestor of Gov. William P. Duvall, of Florida, and of Gen. John Pope Duvall.

[5]BENJAMIN m. [abt 1742] Susanna Tyler
b. 1719 | Daughter of Edw. Tyler of Robert

1 Susanna m. Samuel Tyler, b. 1714
2 Sophia m. Thomas Bott, b. 1716
4 Sarah m. Amos Simpson
6 Mareen b. 1727
7 Charles b. 1729

4th

[2]†WILLIAM m. [abt 1770] Mary Prather
b. 1750, d. 1826, of Frederick Co. | b. 1747, d. 1818, of Frederick Co.

1 Samuel m. Miss Dawson of Charles Co. b. 1747 d. 1821
3 Pannell
4 Mareen m. Miss Howard—moved to Ohio

Note—Samuel was a member of the House of Delegates, was surveyor for Frederick Co. and was the father of Dr. Grafton Duvall of the Maryland Tract.††

[6]GABRIEL m. { 1st [1787] Miss Bries / 2nd [1795] Jane Gibbon }
b. 1752 d. 1844

Note—This was Judge Gabriel Duvall of the U. S. Supreme Court

1 Elizabeth m. Wm. Clark
2 Susanna m. Wm. Higgins
3 Benjamin m. Jemima Taylor
4 Delilah
5 Sarah
7 Edward
8 Isaac
9 Sophia
10 William

5th

[1]JOHN PRATHER m. Sophia Cooke
b. 1777, d. 1840, of Frederick Co. | Daughter of Casper Cooke of Carroll Co.

Note.—Isaac Duvall, son of Benjamin and Jemima Taylor, m. Miss Harding of Montgomery Co. He owned the glass factory at Wellsburg, Va., the first one in the Ohio Valley, and was the father of Gen. Isaac Harding Duvall.

[2]BENJAMIN m. [abt 1805] Rebecca Ijams
b. 1778, d. 1826 | b. 1785, d. 1827

3 Gabriel m. Miss Dean
4 Mary m. Luke Davis
5 Samuel m. Miss Ellison
6 *Daniel m. Hannah Belt
7 Thomas m. Elizabeth Ijams, b. 1789 d. 1869

6th

Note.—All who are named in this generation are of Frederick Co.

[1]WILLIAM TYLER m. { 1st [1846] Mary Ellen Hamrichouse, b. 1826 d. 1860 / 2nd [1860] Ann Rebecca Byers, b. 1835 }
b. 1814, d. 1885

[2]MARY m. Joel Covell
b. —— d. ——

[3]CATHERINE E. m. [1837] GEO. HOOD
b. 1820, d. 1887 | b. 1815, d. 1883

[4]JOHN CASPER m. [1844] Elizabeth Hood
b. 1822, d. 1859 | b. 1824, d. 1886

[4]REBECCA m. Henry Baker
b. 1817, d. 1904 | b. 1818 d. 1896

Annie Eichelberger

1 William
2 Jemima
3 Eliza
4 Frederick
5 Ruth 7 Grafton
8 Sarah 9 Delia
10 Benjamin b. 1827

7th

1 ‡William Caywood
2 Edward Harry d. 1860
3 John Frederick d. 1873
4 Frances Learns d. 1875
5 Mary Ellen
6 Zerian Elizabeth
7 Scott Ellsworth
8 Charles Thomas
9 Katie Tyler d. 1860

1 William Covell d.—
2 Annie Covell
3 John Covell
4 Mary Covell
5 Edward Covell

1 John Hood, M. D. m. Nettie E. Clary
2 Ellen Hood
3 Susan Hood
4 Sophia Hood d. 1870
5 Martha Hood
6 Rachel Tabitha Hood
7 William Albert Hood
8 Mary Catherine Hood
9 George Emory Hood
10 Emma Frances Hood
11 Margaret V. Hood

1 Daniel W.
2 Susan Virginia
3 John Hood d.—
4 William Tyler
5 Catherine Dora

1 Fannie Baker
2 Henry Baker
3 Benjamin Baker
4 Bettie Baker
5 Florence Baker
6 John Edgar Baker

Note.—Compiled and printed in 1902.

†William Duvall commanded the barracks at Frederick during the time the Hessians were confined in them.
††Dr. Grafton Duvall was born 1779, and was educated at St. John's College, Annapolis.
*Daniel Duvall was an officer (Colonel) in the war of 1812.
‡William Caywood Duvall is cashier of the National Bank of Commerce of New York.

Partial Genealogy of the [illegible]

HOMESTEAD OF THE LATE JUDGE GABRIEL DUVALL
Near Collington, Maryland

CPSIA information can be obtained
at www.ICGtesting.com
Printed in the USA
LVHW051908270223
740524LV00037B/1530

9 781015 302648